Frederick Brotherton Meyer

Peace, Perfect Peace

A Portion for the Sorrowing

Frederick Brotherton Meyer

Peace, Perfect Peace
A Portion for the Sorrowing

ISBN/EAN: 9783337778668

Printed in Europe, USA, Canada, Australia, Japan

Cover: Foto ©Thomas Meinert / pixelio.de

More available books at **www.hansebooks.com**

Peace, Perfect Peace

A Portion for the Sorrowing

BY THE REV.

F. B. Meyer, B. A.

Of Christ Church, Westminster Bridge Road, London

New York   Chicago   Toronto

Fleming H. Reveil Company

Publishers Evangelical Literature

Peace, Perfect Peace.

"Thou wilt keep him in perfect peace, whose
mind is stayed on thee."—Isa. xxvi. 3.

Peace, perfect peace, in this dark
    world of sin:
The blood of Jesus whispers peace
    within.

Peace, perfect peace, by thronging
    duties pressed:
To do the will of Jesus, this is rest.

Peace, perfect peace, with sorrows
    surging round:
On Jesus' bosom nought but calm is
    found.

Peace, perfect peace, our future all
    unknown:
Jesus we know, and He is on the
    throne.

Peace, perfect peace, death shadow-
    ing us and ours:
Jesus has vanquished death and all
    its powers.

It is enough: earth's struggles soon
    shall cease,
And Jesus call us to heaven's perfect
    peace.

Bishop E. H. Bickersteth.

I

PEACE, PERFECT PEACE!

"PEACE, perfect peace!" What music there is in the words! The very mention of them fills the heart with longings which cry out for satisfaction, and will not be comforted. Sometimes, indeed, we may succeed in hushing them for a little, as a mother does a fretful child; but soon they will break out again with bitter and insatiable desire. Our nature sighs for rest, as the ocean shell, when placed to the ear, seems to sigh

for the untroubled depths of its
native home.

There is peace in those silent
depths of space, blue for very dis·
tance, which bend with such gentle
tenderness over our fevered, troubled
lives. There is peace in the repose
of the unruffled waters of the moun·
tain lake, sheltered from the winds
by the giant cliffs around. There is
peace at the heart of the whirlwind
which sweeps across the desert waste
in whirling fury. The peace of a
woodland dell, of a highland glen, of
a summer landscape, all touch us.
And is there none for us, whose
nature is so vast, so composite, so
wonderful?

There is. As Jacob lay adying in
his hieroglyphed chamber, not far
from the Pyramids, his face shad-
owed by approaching death, but
aglow with the light of the world

to which he was going, he told how
Shiloh, the Peaceful One, the Peace-
giver, should come to give peace to
men. Weary generations passed by
and still he came not, until at length
there stood among men One, whose
outward life was full of sorrow and
toil; but whose sweet calm face
mirrored the unbroken peace that
reigned within His breast. He was
the promised Peace-giver. He had
peace in Himself; for he said, " My
peace." He had the power of passing that peace on to others; for He
said, "My peace I *give* unto you."
Why should not each reader of these
lines receive the peace which Jesus
had Himself, and which He waits to
give to every longing and recipient
heart ?

A poor woman timidly asked the
gardener of a gentleman's hothouse
if he would sell her *just one bunch of*

grapes for her dying child. He gruffly threatened to summon the police unless she quickly left the place. But as she sadly turned away, she was recalled by a girlish voice, bidding her stay, asking her story, and insisting on her having as many bunches as she could carry with her. And when she offered her few halfpence in return, she was met by the sweet, laughing answer, "Nay, my poor woman. this is my father's hothouse; we don't sell grapes here, but we are very pleased to *give* them; take them and welcome, for your dying child." It is so that Jesus *gives* His peace to all weary, tired ones. Why not to you?

His peace is *perfect* (Isa. xxvi. 3). Unbroken by storms. Uninvaded by the rabble rout of care. Unreached by the highest surges of sorrow. Unstained by the contaminating touch of sin. The very same peace that reigns in Heaven, where all is perfect and complete.

His peace is *as a river* (Isa. xlviii. 18). The dweller on its banks in time of drought is well supplied with water. It is flowing at early dawn, as he goes to his daily toil. It is there in the scorching noon. It is there when the stars shine, hushing him to sleep with the melody of its waves. When he was a child, he plucked the flowerets on its banks; and when his foot shall tread its banks never more, his children's children shall come to drink its streams. Think, too, how it broadens and deepens and fills up, in its onward journey, and from its source to the boundless, infinite sea. So may our peace be, abiding and growing with our years.

His peace is *great* (Isa. liv, 13).

The mountains may depart and the hills be removed, yet shall it abide. Its music is louder than the tumult of the storm. Learn the lesson of the Lake of Galilee; that the peace which is in the heart of Jesus, and which He gives to His own, can quell the greatest hurricane that ever swept down the mountain ravine and spent itself on the writhing waters beneath. For when the Master arose and rebuked the wind and said unto the sea, " Peace, be still," the winds ceased and there was a great calm. " Great peace have they which love Thy law, and nothing shall offend them."

His peace is *compatible with much tribulation* (John xvi. 33). If we never find our path dipping down into the sunless valley, we may seriously question whether we have not missed our way to the Celestial City.

The road to the Mount of Ascension
invariably passes through the shad-
owed Garden of Gethsemane, and
over the steep ascent of Calvary,
and then down into the Garden of
the Grave. "We must through
much tribulation enter into the kingdom of God." But amidst it all it
is possible to be kept in unbroken
peace, like that which possessed the
heart of Jesus, enabling Him calmly
to work a miracle of healing amid
the tumult of His arrest.

His peace *passeth all understanding*
(Phil. iv. 7). It cannot be put into
words. It defies analysis. It must
be felt to be understood. The thing
most like it is the gladsomeness of a
child in its father's home, where
wealth and love and wise nurture
combine to supply all its need ; but
even that falls short of the glorious
reality. "Eye hath not seen, nor

13

ear heard, neither have entered into
the heart of man, the things which
God hath prepared for them that
love Him ; but God hath revealed
them unto us by His Spirit. We
have the mind of Christ." And
(bringing out the deep meaning of
the Greek) we may say, that this
peace will *sentinel* our hearts and
minds, going to and fro, like a sentry
before a palace, to keep off the in-
truders that would break in upon the
sacred enclosure. Oh that we might
be ever protected by a guardianship
so benign and watchful and invul-
nerable to attack.

There are a few conditions, how-
ever, which demand our careful
thought.

1. THE BASIS OF PEACE IS THE
BLOOD.—" He made peace by the
Blood of His Cross " (Col. i, 20).
We sometimes hear men speak of

making their peace with God. But that is wholly needless. Peace has been made. When Jesus died on the Cross, He did all that needed to be done, and all that could be done, so far as God was concerned, in order to bring peace to men. Nothing more is requisite, save to lay aside fear and suspicion, and to accept the peace which He now sweetly and freely offers. " God was in Christ, reconciling the world unto Himself, not imputing their trespasses unto them . . . . now be ye reconciled" (2 Cor. v. 19, 20).

There were many obstacles to our peace, but they have been entirely met and put out of the way. God's Holy Justice, which would pursue us with its drawn sword, can say nothing against us, because it has been more vindicated in the death of the Son of God, than it could

nave been in the perdition of myriads of worlds. The broken law,
which might press its claims, is si-
lenced by the full and complete satisfaction rendered it in the obedience
and death of the Law-giver Himself.
Conscience even, with its long and
bitter record of repeated sin, feels
able to appropriate forgiveness without scruple or alarm; because it un-
derstands that God can be just, and
yet justify the believer in Jesus.
"Who is he that condemneth? It
is Christ that died; yea, rather that
is risen again; who is even at the
right hand of God; who also maketh
intercession for us."

On the evening of His resurrection, our Lord entered through the
unopened doors into the chamber
where His disciples were cowering
for fear of the Jews. His benediction, *Peace be unto you*, fell on their

ears like the chime of bells amid the storm of Friburg's organ. But He did not rest satisfied with this. Indeed, His words alone would have been in vain. But when He had so said, He showed unto them His hands and His side, fresh from the cross, with the marks of spear and nails, so that He stood amid them like a lamb, "as it had been slain." Do you wonder that they were glad? The heart must always be glad when it learns the sure basis of Peace in the Blood shed on the Cross. Rest on that precious Blood; make much of it; remember that God sees it, even if you do not; be sure that it pleads through the ages, with undiminished efficacy; and be at peace.

2. The Method of Peace is by Faith in God's Word.—How many Christians miss God's peace because they look into their hearts to see

how they feel. If they feel right and happy they are at peace. But if mists veil the inner sky, or the body is out of health, or the temperature of the heart is low, they become sad and depressed, and ill at ease. Peace has taken its flight. This will never do. Life is one long torture thus. This is not the blessed life which Jesus came to give us. To live like this is indeed to miss the prize of our high calling and to cast discredit on His dear Name. *If you seek peace through the medium of feeling you will seek it in vain.* It may come as a wayfaring man for a night, but it will not tarry. It may visit you like a transient gleam over the hillside, but it will be only a tiny break be· tween long leagues of cloud. There is a more excellent way. Take up the Bible, the Word of God *to you.* Turn to some of the texts, which

18

shine in its firmament, as stars of the first magnitude in the midnight sky. Consider, for instance, words like these. Ponder them well. Seek not for frames, or feelings, or even for faith, but concentrate your mind and heart upon their mighty mean-ing.

" Whosoever *believeth* in Him shall not perish, but have everlasting life " (John iii. 16).

" He that *heareth* My word, and *believeth* on Him that sent Me, hath everlasting life, and shall not come into condemnation, but is passed from death unto life " (John v. 24).

" By Him, *all that believe* are justi-fied from all things " (Acts xiii. 39).

" The blood of Jesus Christ cleans-eth from *all* sin " (1 John i. 7).

What do these words mean ? Can they mean one straw less than they say ? And if they are as they seem,

19

is it not clear that directly you *believe* you stand before God as a reconciled, accepted and beloved, child ?

What is it to believe? It is to look up to Jesus, as a personal Saviour, handing over to Him the whole burden of your soul, for time and eternity; sure that He takes what you give, at the moment of your giving it, even though you feel no immediate peace or joy. Belief in the outset is *trust*.

" *Your faith is so weak.*" But that does not matter, because there is not a word said about the amount of faith. The greatest faith could not make you more secure. The smallest faith cannot put you outside the circle of blessing; because the word, *believeth*, is so delightfully vague. Faith as grain of mustard seed can move a mountain equally

20

with faith as a walnut shell. Faith
that can only touch the garment hem
gets a blessing which those who
press may lose.

" *You are not sure if you have the
right faith.*" But all faith, any
faith, is the right faith. There are
not many sorts of faith. The faith
that can only lay down its weary
weight on Jesus; the faith that *tries*
to look to Him ; the faith that stag-
gers toward Him, and drops into His
arms; the faith that cannot cling because its hands are so weak, but
which calls to Him, believing that
He can save,—*That* is all the faith
you need, and having it you are
saved.

" *But do you not feel saved.*" And
who said that that was an essential
condition of salvation? Remember
that it is one thing to be saved, and
quite another to feel it. The one

may exist without the other; and
there are no doubt very many, who
are certainly the children of God, but
who have never had the sweet assur-
ance of salvation, which is the seal
of the Spirit, the blossom of grace,
the kiss of God. *Directly you look
to Jesus, you are saved, whether you
feel it or not.* Don't think about
your feelings; don't think about
your faith ; look to Jesus, and reckon
that God will keep His word, and
save you.

The result of all this must inevitably be peace. Let Satan from without join with the timid heart within
in threatening disaster ; faith simply
turns to the Word of God, and putting its finger on one of His exceed-
ing great and precious promises, re-
plies, " This must fail ere I can perish ; but I know whom I have believed, and am persuaded He will

22

keep His word, and that He is able to keep that which I have committed unto Him."

3. THE SECRET OF PEACE IS THE CONSTANT REFERENCE OF ALL TO THE CARE OF GOD.—"Be anxious in nothing; but in everything by prayer and supplication with thanksgiving let your requests be made known unto God; and the peace of God shall guard your hearts and your thoughts in Christ Jesus" (Phil. iv. 6, 7). Acid dropped on steel, and allowed to remain there, will soon corrode it. And if we allow worries, anxieties, careworn questioning to brood in our hearts, they will soon break up our peace, as swarms of tiny gnats will make a paradise un-inhabitable.

There is only one thing that we can do. We must hand them over to Jesus just as they occur. It will not do to wait until the day is done, but in the midst of its busy rush, whenever we are conscious of having lost our peace, we should stand still and ask the cause, and then lift up our hearts and pass it off into the care of our loving and compassionate Lord. "'Tis enough that He should care, why should we the burden bear?"

Ah! what would not our days become, if only we could acquire this blessed habit? We look so weighted, and lead such burdened lives, because we do not trust Jesus with all the little worries of daily life. There is nothing small to Him if it hinders our peace. And when once you have handed aught to Him, refuse to take it back again, and treat the tendency to do so as a temptation to which you dare not give away, no, not for a moment.

Care comes from many sources. Our daily food, our dear ones, our worldly prospects, our Christian work, our pathway in life, our growth in the Divine Life—all these contribute their quota to the total sum. Let us take them all, and lay them down at Jesus' feet, and leave them there; and then live looking to Him to do in us, with us, through us, for us, just as He will. And as we give Him our cares, He will give us His peace, and as He does so He will whisper, "My peace I give unto you, let not your heart be troubled, neither let it be afraid."

There is a remarkable text in Isaiah, which teaches us that the Government should be upon the shoulders of Jesus Christ; and that when it is so, there is no end to the increase of Peace. " *Of the increase of His government and peace there shall be no end*" (ix. 7). Surely these glorious words refer, not only to the government of a nation, but of each individual life also, and they are very searching.

Where is the government of our lives? Is it in our own hands? Then we must not be surprised, if our hearts are like the troubled sea, when it cannot rest. We are out of harmony with God, and with His will, which must be done whether in us or in spite of us. There can be no Peace, because there is perpetual clashing and rebellion.

But directly we put the government of our lives, down to their smallest details, into the hands of the Lord Jesus; then we enter into His own infinite Peace. And as His government is extended over our hearts and lives, so does our Peace extend, as when the blessed light of dawn spreads like a benediction through the world.

"In Me ye shall have peace." 'Twas our Saviour who said those words. Let us abide in Him. Let us live in Him. Let us walk in Him. Let us make of Him the secret place unto which we may continually resort. And as we are joined to Him, in the intimacy of deepest union, the peace that fills His heart, like a Pacific ocean, shall begin to flow into ours, until they are filled with the very fulness of God ; and the peace of God, like a dove, with fluttering wings, shall settle down upon our hearts, and make them its home forevermore.

That this Peace may become the blessed portion of you, my reader, is my sincere wish.

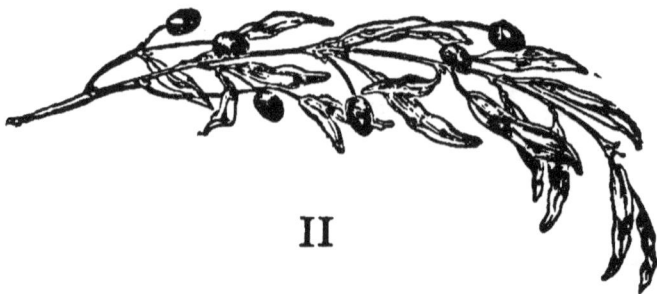

II

HOW TO BEAR SORROW

YOU are passing through a time of deep sorrow. The love on which you were trusting has suddenly failed you, and dried up like a brook in the desert—now a dwindling stream, then shallow pools, and at last drought. You are always listening for footsteps that do not come, waiting for a word that is not spoken, pining for a reply that tarries overdue.

Perhaps the savings of your life have suddenly disappeared ; instead of helping others you must be helped, or you must leave the warm nest

where you have been sheltered from
life's storms to go alone into an un-
friendly world; or you are suddenly
called to assume the burden of some
other life, taking no rest for yourself
till you have steered it through dark
and difficult seas into the haven.
Your health, or sight, or nervous
energy is failing; you carry in yourself the sentence of death; and the
anguish of anticipating the future is
almost unbearable. In other cases
there is the sense of recent loss
through death, like the gap in the
forest-glade, where the woodsman has
lately been felling trees.

At such times life seems almost
insupportable. Will every day be
as long as this? Will the slow-mov-
ing hours ever again quicken their
pace? Will life ever array itself in
another garb than the torn autumn
remnants of past summer glory?

29

Hath God forgotten to be gracious? Hath He in anger shut up His tender mercies? Is His mercy clean gone forever?

This road has been trodden by myriads.—When you think of the desolating wars which have swept through every century and devastated every land; of the expeditions of the Nimrods, the Nebuchadnezzars, the Timours, the Napoleons of history; of the merciless slave-trade, which has never ceased to decimate Africa; and of all the tyranny, the oppression, the wrong which the weak and defenseless have suffered at the hands of their fellows; of the unutterable sorrows of women and children, surely you must see that by far the larger number of our race have passed through the same bitter griefs as those which rend your heart. Jesus Christ Himself trod this diffi-

cult path, leaving traces of His blood
on its flints; and apostles, prophets,
confessors, and martyrs have passed
by the same way. It is comforting
to know that others have traversed
the same dark valley and that the
great multitudes which stand before
the Lamb, wearing palms of victory,
came out of great tribulation. Where
they were we are; and, by God's
grace, where they are we shall be.

Do not talk about punishment.—
You may talk of chastisement or cor-
rection, for our Father deals with us
as with sons; or you may speak of
reaping the results of mistakes and
sins dropped as seeds into life's fur-
rows in former years; or you may
have to bear the consequences of the
sins and mistakes of others; but do
not speak of punishment. Surely
all the guilt and penalty of sin were
laid on Jesus, and he put them away

forever. His were the stripes and the chastisement of our peace. If God punishes us for our sins, it would seem that the sufferings of Christ were incomplete; and if He once began to punish us, life would be too short for the infliction of all that we deserve. Besides, how could we explain the anomalies of life, and the heavy sufferings of the saints as compared with the gay life of the ungodly? Surely, if our sufferings were penal, there would be a reversal of these lots.

Sorrow is a refiner's crucible.—It may be caused by the neglect or cruelty of another, by circumstances over which the sufferer has no control, or as the direct result of some dark hour in the long past; but, inasmuch as God has permitted it to come, it must be accepted as His appointment, and considered as the furnace by which He is searching, testing, probing, and purifying the soul. Suffering searches us as fire does metals. We think we are fully for God, until we are exposed to the cleansing fire of pain; then we discover, as Job did, how much dross there is in us, and how little real patience, resignation, and faith. Nothing so detaches us from the things of this world, the life of sense, the birdlime of earthly affections. There is probably no other way by which the power of the self-life can be arrested, that the life of Jesus may be manifested in our mortal flesh.

But God always keeps the discipline of sorrow in His own hands.—Our Lord said, " My Father is the husbandman." His hand holds the pruning-knife; His eye watches the crucible; His gentle touch is on the

3

pulse while the operation is in progress. He will not allow even the devil to have his own way with us. As in the case of Job, so always. The moments are carefully allotted. The severity of the test is exactly determined by the reserves of grace and strength which are lying unrecognized within, but will be sought for and used beneath the severe pressure of pain. He holds the winds in His fist, and the waters in the hollow of His hand. He dare not risk the loss of that which has cost Him the blood of His son. "God is faithful, who will not suffer you to be *tried* above that you are able."

In sorrow the Comforter is near.— "Very present in time of trouble." He *sits* by the crucible, as a Refiner of silver, regulating the heat, marking every change, waiting patiently for the scum to float away, and His

34

own face to be mirrored in clear, translucent metal. No earthly friend may tread the winepress with you, but the Saviour is there, His garments stained with the blood of the grapes of your sorrow. Dare to re-peat it often, though you do not feel it, and though Satan insists that God has left you, " *Thou art with me.*" Mention His name again and again, "*Jesus*, JESUS, Thou art with me." So you will become conscious that He is there.

When friends come to console you they talk of time's healing touch, as though the best balm for sorrow were to forget, or in their well-meant kind-ness they suggest travel, diversion, amusement, and show their inability to appreciate the black night that hangs over your soul, so you turn from them, sick at heart, and pre-pared to say, as Job of his, " Miserable comforters are ye all;" but all the while Jesus is nearer than they are, understanding how they wear you, knowing each throb of pain, touched by fellow-feeling, silent in a love too full to speak, waiting to comfort from hour to hour as a mother her weary, suffering babe.

Be sure to study the art of this Divine comfort, that you may be able to comfort them that are in any affliction with the comfort with which you yourself have been comforted of God (2 Cor. i. 4). There can be no doubt that some trials are permitted to come to us, as to our Lord, for no other reason than that by means of them we should become able to give sympathy and succor to others. And we should watch with all care each symptom of the pain, and each prescription of the Great Physician, since, in all probability, at some

future time, we shall be called to
minister to those passing through
similar experiences. Thus we learn
by the things that we suffer, and, being made perfect, become authors of
priceless and eternal help to souls in
agony.

*Do not shut yourself up with your
sorrow.*—A friend, in the first anguish
of bereavement, wrote, saying that
he must give up the Christian ministries in which he had delighted; and
I replied immediately, urging him
not to do so, because there is no
solace for heart-pain like ministry.
The temptation of great suffering is
toward isolation, withdrawal from
the life of men, sitting alone, and
keeping silence. Do not yield to it.
Break through the icy chains of re-
serve, if they have already gathered.
Arise, anoint your head, and wash
your face; go forth to do your duty,

with willing though chastened steps. Selfishness, of every kind, in its activities, or its introspection, is a hurtful thing, and shuts out the help and love of God. Sorrow is apt to be selfish. The soul, occupied with its own griefs, and refusing to be comforted, becomes presently a Dead Sea, full of brine and salt, over which birds do not fly, and beside which no green thing grows. And thus we miss the very lesson that God would teach us. His constant war is against the self-life, and every pain He inflicts is to lessen its hold on us. But we may thwart His purpose, and extract poison from His gifts, as men get opium and alcohol from innocent plants.

A Hindoo woman, the beautiful Eastern legend tells us, lost her only child. Wild with grief, she implored a prophet to give back her little one to her love. He looked at her for a long while tenderly, and said, " Go, my daughter, bring me a handful of rice from a house into which Death has never entered, and I will do as thou desirest." The woman at once began her search. She went from dwelling to dwelling, and had no difficulty in obtaining what the prophet specified ; but when they had granted it, she inquired, " Are you all here around the hearth—father, mother, children—none missing ? " But the people invariably shook their heads with sighs and looks of sadness ; for far and wide as she wandered, there was always some vacant seat by the hearth. And gradually, as she passed on, the narrator says, the waves of her grief subsided before the spectacle of sorrow everywhere, and her heart, ceasing to be occupied with its own selfish pang, flowing out in strong yearnings of sympathy with the universal suffering, tears of anguish softened into tears of pity, passion melted away in compassion, she forgot herself in the general interest, and found redemption in redeeming.

Do not chide yourself for feeling strongly.—Tears are natural. Jesus wept. A thunderstorm without rain is fraught with peril; the pattering raindrops cool the air, and relieve the overcharged atmosphere. The swollen brooks indicate that the snows are melting on the hills and spring is near. " Daughters of Jerusalem," said our Lord, " weep for yourselves and your children." To bear sorrow with dry eyes and stolid heart may befit a Stoic, but not a Christian. We have no need to rebuke fond nature crying for its mate, its lost joy, the touch of the vanished hand, the sound of the voice that is still, provided only that the will is resigned. This is the one consideration for those who suffer—*Is the will right?* If it isn't, God himself cannot comfort. If it is, then the path will inevitably lead from the valley of the shadow of death to the banqueting table and the overflowing cup.

Many say : I cannot feel resigned. It is bad enough to have my grief to bear, but I have this added trouble, that I cannot *feel* resigned. My invariable reply is : you probably never can feel resignation, but you can *will* it. The Lord Jesus, in the Garden of Gethsemane, has shown us how to suffer. He chose his Father's will. Though Judas, prompted by Satan, was the instrument for mixing the cup and placing it to the Saviour's lips, He looked right beyond him to the Father, who permitted him to work his cruel way, and said: "The cup that My Father giveth Me to drink, shall I not drink it?" And He said repeatedly, "If this cup may not pass from Me, except I drink it, Thy will be done." He gave up His own way and will, saying, "I will Thy will, O My Father; Thy will, and not Mine, be done."

Let all sufferers who read these lines go apart and dare to say the same words: "Thy will, and not mine; Thy will be done in the earth of my life, as in the heaven of Thy purpose; I choose Thy will." Say this thoughtfully and deliberately, not because you can feel it, but because you will it; not because the way of the cross is pleasant, but because it must be right. Say it repeatedly, whenever the surge of pain sweeps through you, whenever

the wound begins to bleed afresh:
Not my will, but Thine be done.
Dare to say Yes to God. "Even so,
Father, for so it seemeth good in Thy
sight."

And so you will be led to feel that
all is right and well; and a great
calm will settle down on your heart,
a peace that passeth understanding,
a sense of rest, which is not incon-
sistent with suffering, but walks in
the midst of it as the three young
men in the fiery furnace, to whom
the burning coals must have been
like the dewy grass of a forest-glade.
"The doctor told us my little child
was dying. I felt like a stone. But
in a moment I seemed to give up my
hold on her. She appeared no
longer mine, but God's."

Be sure to learn God's lessons.—
Each sorrow carries at its heart a
germ of holy truth, which if you get

and sow in the soil of your heart
will bear harvests of fruit, as seed-
corns from mummy-cases fruit in
English soil. God has a meaning in
each blow of His chisel, each incision
of His knife. He knows the way
that He takes. But His object is
not always clear to us.

In suffering and sorrow God
touches the minor chords, develops
the passive virtues, and opens to
view the treasures of darkness, the
constellations of promise, the rain-
bow of hope, the silver light of the
covenant. What is character without sympathy, submission, patience,
trust, and hope that grips the unseen
as an anchor? But these graces are
only possible through sorrow. Sorrow is a garden, the trees of which
are laden with the peaceable fruits of
righteousness; do not leave it without bringing them with you. Sor-

row is a mine, the walls of which glisten with precious stones; be sure and do not retrace your steps into daylight without some specimens. Sorrow is a school. You are sent to sit on its hard benches and learn from its black-lettered pages lessons which will make you wise forever; do not trifle away your chance of graduating there. Miss Havergal used to talk of " turned lessons! "

Count on the afterward.—God will not always be causing grief. He traverses the dull brown acres with His plough, seaming the yielding earth, that He may be able to cast in the precious grain. Believe that in days of sorrow He is sowing light for the righteous, and gladness for the upright in heart. Look forward to the reaping. Anticipate the joy which is set before you, and shall flood your heart with minstrel notes

45

when patience has had her perfect
work.

You will live to recognize the
wisdom of God's choice for you.
You will one day see that the thing
you wanted was only second best.
You will be surprised to remember
that you once nearly broke your
heart and spilt the wine of your life,
for what would never have satisfied
you, if you had caught it, as the
child the butterfly or soap-bubble.
You will meet again your beloved.
You will have again your love. You
will become possessed of a depth of
character, a breadth of sympathy, a
fund of patience, an ability to under-
stand and help others, which, as you
lay them at Christ's feet for Him to
use, will make you glad that you
were afflicted. You will see God's
plan and purpose; you will reap His
harvest; you will behold His face.

and be satisfied. Each wound will have its pearl; each carcass will con-tain a swarm of bees; each foe, like Midian to Gideon, will yield its goodly spoil.

The way of the cross, rightly borne, is the only way to the ever-lasting light. The path that threads the Garden of Gethsemane, and climbs over the hill of Calvary, alone conducts to the visions of the Easter morning and the glories of the Ascension mount. If we will not drink of His cup, or be baptized with His baptism, or fill up that which is behind of His sufferings, we cannot expect to share in the joys of His espousals and the ecstasy of His triumph. But if these conditions are fulfilled, we shall not miss one note in the everlasting song, one element in the bliss that is possible to men.

Remember that somehow suffering rightly borne enriches and helps mankind.—The death of Hallam was the birthday of Tennyson's *In Memoriam.* The cloud of insanity that brooded over Cowper gave us, *God moves in a mysterious way.* Milton's blindness taught him to sing of *Holy Light, offspring of heaven's firstborn.* Rist used to say, " The dear cross has pressed many songs out of me." And it is probable that none rightly suffer anywhere without contributing something to the alleviation of human grief, to the triumph of good over evil, of love over hate, and of light over darkness.

If you believed this, could you not bear to suffer? Is not the chief misery of all suffering its loneliness, and perhaps its apparent aimlessness? Then dare to believe that no man dieth to himself. Fall into the ground, bravely and cheerfully, to die; if you refuse this, you will abide alone, but if you yield to it, you will bear fruit which will sweeten the lot and strengthen the life of others who will never know your name, or stop to thank you for your help.

III

THE BLESSED DEAD

ON the quay of an obscure Norwegian town I once saw a parting between a little group of emigrants, about to try their fortunes in a strange and distant land, and their friends and relatives, who gathered to bid them a last adieu. They were altogether of the poorest class, their goods in clumsy boxes, or clumsier canvas; but that nature spoke, through their evident grief, which makes us all kin. But the chief point of interest was the wistful eagerness with which the eyes of those on shore followed the wake of the retreating vessel, as though they would fain pierce the parting veil of distance, and see the land into which their dear ones went, perhaps never to return.

So is it often as we gather around the spot from which some beloved soul is about to depart into the unseen. Whither does it go? What does it behold? Whence comes the light which illumines the wan and pallid features, till they seem already transfigured into the likeness of an angel? We gaze where we almost expect to see an open heaven, but all is opaque and dark; and we turn away to take up our lonely path, and to wonder with a great awe as to what is really involved in this great and solemn mystery, which we call

Death, but which angels know as Birth.

Obviously, in death, there is no break in the soul's consciousness. The life of the spirit is altogether independent of the body in which it dwells. The signal-box may be in ruins, and yet the operator may be within—as clear in thought and quick of hand as in the day when all was new. It oftens happens, when the body is at the point of death, that the spirit reveals itself in undiminished splendor, and flashes forth in thoughts that can never be forgotten, and words that can never die. And does not this prove, beyond doubt, that the spirit is only a lodger in the body, and when the house of its tabernacle is broken up, it is not affected, but simply passes out to find some other and more lasting home. "We know that if the earthly house of our tabernacle " (this bodily frame) " be dissolved, we have a house not made with hands, eternal, in the heavens " (2 Cor. v. 1).

This conclusion, arrived at on merely natural grounds, is substantiated by all the references of the New Testament. There is no shadow of warrant for the idea (held by some) that there is a pause in our consciousness, a parenthesis in our existence, between death and the resurrection. " To depart," said St. Paul, " is to be with Christ, which is far better " (Phil. i. 23). But surely it could not have been far better to pass into a sort of sleep! Better to live on in this mortal life, amid the acutest sufferings, and to have the presence of Christ, than to lose that presence during centuries of unconsciousness.

" To be absent from the body," he

said again, " is to be present with the Lord " (2 Cor. v. 8). The moment of absence is the moment of presence. As the spirit withdraws itself from the body, closing blinds and shutters as it retires, it immediately presents itself in the presence of the King, to go no more out for ever.

" Them also which sleep in Jesus will God bring with Him " (*i. e.,* with the Lord on His second coming for His own); "and the dead in Christ shall rise first " (1 Thess. iv. 14, 16). Clearly, then, those who have fallen asleep in Jesus (this is the constant phrase used by the Apostles for the death of the believer) have gone to be with Christ, or they could not be said to return with Him ; and their spirit-life must be independent of their bodies, which will only be raised when the angel· trumpet calls them from the grave.

54

And the beloved Apostle distinctly closes the door against all further doubt and questioning on this matter, when he says, " I heard a voice from heaven, saying unto me, Write, Blessed are the dead which die in the Lord from henceforth " (Rev. xiv. 13). What can those two last words mean except that the blessed rest of the beloved dead dates from the moment that they have died in the Lord?

Death is not a state, but an act; not a condition, but a passage. In this it finds its true analogy in birth, by which we entered upon a new stage of existence. In death we are born out of the darkness and constraints of this mortal life into the freedom and light of Heaven. So Christ was called " the *firstborn* from among the dead." A moment's anguish; a wrench; a step; a transition; a breaking through the thin veil, which hangs between two worlds; a stepping across the boundary line—such is death. And the soul carries with it across that boundary line its freight of thought and life, to pursue its continuity of being and love and purpose in an unbroken and uninterrupted course. The dead are those who have died, and are living for evermore an intense bright life (Ps. xxi. 6).

OF COURSE, THEN, OUR DEAR AND SAINTED DEAD LOVE US AS THEY EVER DID. Their love to us was a part of their existence, woven into their innermost being, as warp with woof. It was not a property of the body which they have left behind, but of themselves. And we cannot think of them as being the same beings as they were without that love. If, as we have seen, the spirit carries

on its life unbroken and unaffected
by its passage from the body, then it
must continue to live on the other
side as on this side. Its love is only
altered in its brilliance and intensity,
not in its objects ; just as a piece of
phosphorus, which burns in ordinary
air, sparkles with unwonted corusca-
tions when suddenly plunged into a
jar of oxygen gas.

Love never dies (1 Cor. xiii.).
Our partial *knowledge* dies amid the
revelations of perfect vision. *Faith*
will be needed no more where we
know as we are known. *Hope* fades
in fruition. But *love* abides for ever.
It never fails. Death may cut off
the interchange of words and acts of
love, but its cold hand cannot touch
that which is Divine origin, eternal
in nature and everlasting in dura-
tion.

That is what we pine to know. **It**

is not the distance that makes our souls faint and fear; we could bear that; but the feeling that perhaps we have lost for ever the love which was the light of our existence, the fire at which we were wont to warm ourselves. Let us know that this is preserved to us still; that they love us still who have left us; that their thoughts still enfold us in tender embracements, and follow us in our wanderings, and hover over us like ministering angels—then we can afford to be without their presence; nay, we gladly resign them, because they are happier where they are than we could ever have made them.

If your child were to cross the seas, and sojourn for all coming years of life amid strange surroundings and foreign tongues, would you expect it to cease to love? Did Joseph forget his father or brothers when suffering in the prison, or reigning on the throne? Did Moses cease to love his mother, when for forty years he dwelt in the palace of the Pharaohs? Did the little maid forget her home when she was transported to the halls of the warrior Naaman? And why should we suppose that those forget us who have passed into the City of God, where the soul only loses its grossness and denseness, but where all that is true and noble and lovely reveals itself in fellowship with its fellows?

Oh, press this thought to your innermost soul—that those whom you have "loved long since and lost awhile" love you still, care for you still, with a warmth of affection which kindles into an intenser brilliance, as they come nearer to the heart of the Eternal Father, the Source and Sun of Love. And

in this love they wait for us. They
cannot attain their full consumma-
tion and bliss until we, too, emerge
from the shadows of death into the
perfect light of eternity; so only
shall love be satisfied.

But if the love of earth be preserved on the other side, will they
not suffer more pain than pleasure,
more anguish for those who are over-
come by evil than joy for those who
conquer? Yet, surely, Heaven cannot be a place of selfish enjoyment.
The very essence of its bliss will be
in thought and care for others. Its
happy residents cannot be oblivious
to the travail that rends the heart of
its Master for the world He loves,
and the Church, His bride. Death
will only bring them into closer sympathy with Him in His great plans
of redemption, and may reveal to
them considerations and possibilities

which will mitigate their anxiety, and enable them to wait the unfolding of His plans for those whom they have left behind. " Here is the patience and the faith of the saints."

OUR SAINTED DEAD WILL BE CAPABLE OF RECOGNITION. Of what use would it be if they were so changed that we could not know them? Even if they were the same in essence they would not be the same to us. Of course they will not wear the body of mortality, racked with pain, dissolved in death. " Flesh and blood cannot inherit the kingdom of heaven." " This corruptible must put on incorruption. This mortal must put on immortality." But the resurrection body, as is proved by the story of the Forty Days, though in many respects different, is so nearly like the body of our present life that it can be recognized, not only in the general outline, but by the very intonation of the voice, speaking the dear old familiar names of the past.

Mary did not recognize Christ at first, because she would not lift her tear-blinded eyes from the grave where she had seen His sacred body laid; but the tones of His voice recalled her from her sad reverie, and made her start with recognition. The two who walked to Emmaus would have known Him if their eyes had not been holden. And when repeated opportunities were given to the rest to verify Him as the same Jesus with Whom they had spent three years of blessed fellowship, they knew Him, and "were glad when they saw the Lord." Those alone did not see Him whose senses were beclouded by unbelief or earthliness.

So shall it be with all who belong

to Him. His resurrection body is a pattern of ours. "He shall fashion anew the body of our humiliation, that it may be conformed to the body of His glory" (Phil. iii. 21). The spirit will be robed in an ethereal, spiritual body, obedient to its every behest, the meet vehicle of its bright and blessed life; but that glorious body will, in its tones and look and acts (John xxi. 7), recall the loved spirit with which our heart was entwined.

Sometimes, when reaching a crowded railway station, we have been refreshed by seeing the faces of those we know and love, who have come to meet us with their welcome. So Paul felt as his weary journey approached its end at Appii-Forum. But what will it not be to be greeted on the other side by familiar faces, and well-known voices, and tokens by which to recognize the dearly loved! Yet this is what we may expect. We are to be gathered unto our people; a phrase which cannot mean their dust, because the word "buried" is used of this, and, therefore, which must mean their living, loving, recognized, and welcoming presence. Those whom we have befriended will welcome us into eternal habitations. A choral entrance is to be ministered unto us into the home of the saints (Luke xvi. 9; 2 Pet. i. 11).

ONCE MORE: THE BLESSED DEAD ARE NOT FAR AWAY. They are where Jesus is; and since He is here, may they not be here too? Heaven is not "far away," as the children are taught to sing. It is near at hand, within the moment's flash of the spirit's flight. "To-day" (and it was near sunset when the

Speaker said it) " thou shalt be with Me in Paradise." "Absent from the body, present with the Lord." No doubt there are several heavens through which ultimately spirits shall pass in their upward mounting (Eph. iv. 10); but the third chamber of the many mansions, Paradise, where now the blessed dead are gathering, and where they await the resurrection is near, very near (2 Cor. xii. 2, 4). There is but a step between.

The prayer of Jesus was that His Church should be one in the Father and Himself. He made no distinction between those who should have crossed the border line and those still lingering on this side. And thus we may infer that all those who are one with Him are one with each other; and that, when we realize our union with Him most closely, we are warranted also to realize our union with all the Catholic Church in heaven and earth, and especially with our beloved. Moses and Elias met the disciples in the Transfiguration Mount. And saints still meet us when we are nearest Christ. The members of the same body cannot be very far from each other!

Those dissevered by miles of land and sea meet each other in spirit as they gather at the same hour at the Table of the Lord; and those who touch Christ from the heaven side meet us in Him when we touch Him from the earth side. Hallelujah! To the holy soul, not heaven only, but earth, and vale, and hill, and all lovely scenes are thronged with the presence of bright, radiant, and holy spirits, among whom we recognize those who have been ours, and are ours for ever.

And there is this thought also for

those who have lost the child, the
young sweet friend, the bright dear
life from which it seemed so hard to
part. From the moment that death
takes them they cease to grow old;
they always remain to us what they
were in all their radiant beauty.
There is always a child-life in the
house where a child has died, always
merry ringing tones, always soft
caresses, always pretty childish ways.
The other children grow up and pass
out into life and the world; but the
child whom death has taken is always
there, there for ever in unimpaired
beauty and freshness. Oh, Death,
thou angel of God, thou dost seem to
rob us of our treasures, but thou dost
really make them ours for ever in the
dew of an immortal youth, trans-
figuring them with a light that can
never fade from their faces or our
lives; blotting out only what we are

glad to forget, preserving what we loved in imperishable beauty !

The bereaved have often said to me bitterly, " I cannot *feel* resigned ; I know that it must be all right, but I cannot *feel* resigned." But, does God expect us to deny the love He gave us, as it pines for " the touch of the vanished hand, and the sound of the voice that is still"? Jesus wept at the grave of His friend.

There are two kinds of sorrow— the sorrow which misses its companion at every turn, and at each fresh sense of loss weeps bitter tears under a keen sense of pain; and there is the hard, bitter, unresigned, and unsubmissive sorrow, which will not forgive God. It is only the latter of these which is wrong. The first is natural, and there is no cause in it for self-rebuke.

When grief is fresh do not try to

feel resignation, but *will* it. Look up to God, in the first stab of pain, and in all the long weary hours of suffer-ing which follow, and say, " Father, I choose Thy will; I know it is the tenderest and best for my loved one, and for me. Even so, my Father, for so it seemed good in Thy sight; not my will, but Thine be done." And as these words are repeated, and the will offers itself to God, and lays its sacrifice upon the altar, though the hand trembles and the eyes brim with tears, the inward tumult will subside and die down, and the sufferer will come to DELIGHT (not in the sorrow) but, in the Father's appointment, which at first it could only *choose.*

We never know from what lingering suffering, from what bitter grief, from what impending disaster, spiritual or temporal, God has taken our dear ones. He knows best, and has a sufficient reason, and will explain it clearly to us some day. Meanwhile, He Who wounds can heal. He Who takes will Himself fill the vacant place. And He will keep that which we have committed to Him, and give it back to us restored to perfect health and beauty.

God sometimes passes us into the valley of shadow that we may learn the way, and know how to lead others through it into the light. To get comfort we must comfort with the comfort wherewith we ourselves have been comforted. In wiping the tears of others our own will cease to fall.

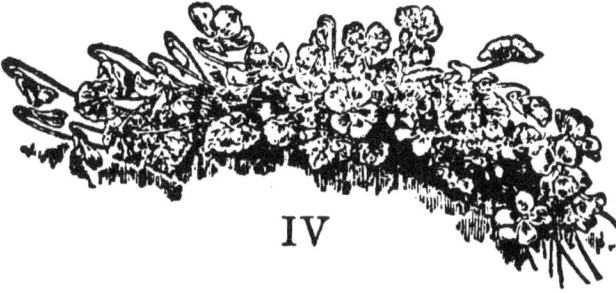

IV

COMFORTED TO COMFORT

" THE God of all comfort, who comforteth us in all our affliction, that
we may be able to comfort them that
are in any affliction, through the
comfort wherewith we ourselves are
comforted of God."—2 Cor. i. 3, 4
(R. V.).

CHILD OF GOD, think it not strange
concerning the fiery trial which tries
thee, as though some strange thing
had happened. Rejoice insomuch as
it is a sure sign that thou art on the
right track. In an unknown coun-
try, a man tells me that I shall pres-

ently pass over a stony bit of road on my way to my abiding-place, and when I come to it, each jolt tells me that I am right. So when a child of God passes through affliction, he is not surprised, but satisfied. He knows that he is right for the gate of pearl, for it is through much tribulation that we enter the kingdom. *Thine afflictions cannot be few.*

Look up. There is thy Father, pure and holy. Thou art to be like Him. But ere thou canst be, thou wilt need the file of the lapidary, the heat of the crucible, the bruising of the flail—not to win thy heaven, but to destroy thine unheavenliness. The spirits gathered there, clad in lustrous white, tell thee that the brilliance of their reward has been in the measure of the vehemence of their sorrows. Be sure, then, that thy Father will put within thy reach a brighter crown, by putting *thee* within the reach of severe affliction.

Look down. Thinkest thou that the prince of hell was pleased, when thou didst forsake him for thy new Master, Christ? Verily not! At the moment of thy conversion thy name was put on the proscribed list, and all the powers of darkness pledged themselves to obstruct thy way. What wonder if affliction comes to thee, as it came to Job, by the permission of heaven, from hell!

Look around. Thou art still in the world that crucified thy Lord, and would do the same again, if He were again to live amidst it. It cannot love thee. It will call thee Beelzebub. It will cast thee out of its synagogue. It will think it a religious act to kill thee. In the world thou shalt have afflictions, though in the midst of them thou mayest be of good cheer.

Look within. What hast thou here but an evil heart, ever chafing against the rule and will of God ; froward, restless, wilful. And in the constant strife between thy will and God's will, what can there be but affliction ? This human life is the college of affliction, whither even the King's son came that He might be a faithful High Priest.

For such as thou art, afflicted one, there is no literature so befitting as the Bible, and in the Bible no part more helpful than this epistle. *Hope* is the keynote of the epistle to the Thessalonians, *joy* of that to the Philippians, *faith* of that to the Romans, *heavenly things* of that to the Ephesians, *affliction* of this. It was written amid afflictions so great, that the Apostle despaired of life.

It is steeped in affliction, as a hand-
herchief with the flowing blood of a
fresh wound. But in this passage,
the Apostle has built for himself a
little chamber of comfort, on the wall
of affliction. Its stones are quarried
from the pit of his own sorrow. In
it he sits and sings, " Blessed be
God; " and into it he bids thee come
till thine affliction be past, and thy
sky is clear again. It is the chamber
of comfort.

When in affliction, mind three
things—Look out for comfort; store
up comfort; pass on the comfort you
get.

(1) LOOK OUT FOR COMFORT.
It will come *certainly*. Wherever
the nettle grows there grows the
dock leaf, and wherever there is a
trial, there is, somewhere at hand, a
sufficient store of comfort, though
our eyes, like Hagar's, are often

holden that we do not see it. But it is as sure as the faithfulness of God.

It will come *proportionately*. God holds a pair of scales. This on the right side called AS, is for thine afflictions; this on the left called SO, is for thy comforts. And the beam is always level. The more thy trial, the more thy comfort. *As* the sufferings of Christ abound in us, *so* our consolation also aboundeth through Christ.

It will come *divinely*. It is well when meeting a friend at the station, to know by what route to expect him, lest he come in on one platform, while we are awaiting him on another. It is equally good to know in what quarter to look for comfort. Shall we look to the hills? No, for in vain is salvation looked for from the hills. Shall we look to man? No, for Job found the best men of his time to be miserable comforters. Shall we look to angels? No, God entrusts angels to fulfill many ministries for us, but never to comfort. This needs a gentler touch than theirs. God dare not entrust it to Gabriel. *He* comforteth those that are cast down. *He* healeth the broken in heart, and bindeth up their wounds.

It will come *mediately.* Our consolation aboundeth *through Christ.* When a bridegroom makes a present to his wife, he puts it in the rarest casket, and sends it by her choicest friend. And when our God comforts us, He adds to the exquisite beauty of His comfort by sending it through the Son of His love.

It will come *directly* through the Holy Ghost, that other Comforter, whom the Saviour gives, and who gives us Him, and in giving us Him gives us all.

It will come *variously*, sometimes by the coming of a beloved Titus, a bouquet, a letter, a message, or a card; sometimes by a promise, laying an ice-cold cloth on our fevered brows; sometimes by God simply coming near. In sore sorrow, *He* comforts best who says least, and who simply draws near, and takes the sufferer's hand, and is silent in his sympathizing love. It is *so* that God comforts. Thou drewest near in the day of mine affliction, Thou saidst, It is I, be not afraid.

II. STORE UP COMFORT. The world is full of comfortless hearts; orphan children crying in the night. Our God pities them, and would comfort them through thee. But ere thou art sufficient for this lofty ministry, thou must be trained. And

78

that He may train thee perfectly,
He puts thee through the very same
afflictions which are wringing human
hearts with aching sorrow. He
makes thus for Himself an opportu-
nity of comforting thee, and of so
teaching thee the divine art of comfort. Watch narrowly how He does
it. Keep a diary if thou wilt, and
note down all the procedure of His
skill. Ponder in thine heart the
length of each splint, the folds of
each bandage, the ministration of
each opiate or cordial or drug. This
will bring a twofold blessing. It
will turn thy thoughts from thy mis-
eries to thine outnumbering mercies ;
and it will take from thee that sense
of useless and aimless existence,
which is often the sufferer's weariest
cross.

Dost thou wonder why thou dost
suffer some special form of sorrow ?

Wait, till ten years are past. I warrant thee, that in that time thou wilt find some, perhaps ten, afflicted as thou art. When thou tellest them how thou hast suffered, and how thou hast been comforted; whilst thou unfoldest thy tale, and seekest to repeat on them the magic spells that have charmed away thy griefs; in their glistening eyes and comforted looks, thou wilt learn why thou hast been afflicted, and thou wilt bless God that thou wert able to comfort others with the comfort wherewith thou thyself hadst been comforted of God. Once more, then, remember to store up an accurate remembrance of the way in which God comforts thee.

III. PASS ON THE COMFORT YOU RECEIVE.—At a railway station a benevolent man found a school-boy crying, because he had not quite

enough to pay his fare; and he re-
membered, suddenly, how, years before, *he* had been in the same plight,
but had been helped by an unknown
friend, and had been enjoined that
some day he should pass that kind-
ness on. Now he saw that the long-
expected moment had come. He
took the weeping boy aside, told him
his story, paid his fare, and asked
him, in his turn, to pass the kindness
on. And as the train moved from
the station, the lad cried cheerily:
" I will pass it on, sir; " so the act
of thoughtful love is being passed
on through our world, nor will it
stay till its ripples have belted the
globe and met again.

" Go thou and do likewise." Is
thy heart comforted? Then be on
the alert to comfort those who are in
any trouble. Thou canst not miss
them; they are not scarce. Thine

own sad past will make thee quick
to detect them, where others might
miss them. If thou findest them not,
seek them ; the wounded heart goes
alone to die. Sorrow shuns society.
Thou shouldest constantly seek from
the Man of Sorrows Himself, di-
rections as to where the sorrowing
bide. He knows their haunts, from
which they have cried to Him. And
when thou comest where they are, do
for them as the Good Samaritan did
for thee, when He bound up thy
wounds, pouring in oil and wine.
Comfort them with the comfort
wherewith thou thyself hast been
comforted of God.

www.ingramcontent.com/pod-product-compliance
Lightning Source LLC
Chambersburg PA
CBHW022140090426
42742CB00010B/1337